Electricity

Kaite Goldsworthy

www.av2books.com

AV² provides enriched content that supplements and complements this book. Weigl's AV² books strive to create inspired learning and engage young minds in a total learning experience.

Your AV² Media Enhanced books come alive with...

Audio
Listen to sections of the book read aloud.

Key Words
Study vocabulary, and complete a matching word activity.

Video
Watch informative video clips.

Quizzes
Test your knowledge.

Go to www.av2books.com, and enter this book's unique code.

Embedded Weblinks
Gain additional information for research.

Slide Show
View images and captions, and prepare a presentation.

BOOK CODE

W801786

AV² **by Weigl** brings you media enhanced books that support active learning.

Try This!
Complete activities and hands-on experiments.

... and much, much more!

Published by AV² by Weigl
350 5th Avenue, 59th Floor
New York, NY 10118
Website: www.av2books.com   www.weigl.com

Library of Congress Cataloging-in-Publication Data

Goldsworthy, Kaite.
 Electricity / Kaite Goldsworthy.
    p. cm. -- (Physical science)
 Includes index.
 ISBN 978-1-61690-727-3 (hardcover : alk. paper) -- ISBN 978-1-61690-731-0 (softcover : alk. paper)
 1. Electricity--Juvenile literature. I. Title.
 QC527.2.G65 2012
 537--dc22
                              2011002293

Printed in the United States of America in North Mankato, Minnesota
1 2 3 4 5 6 7 8 9 15 14 13 12 11

052011
WEP37500

Project Coordinator Aaron Carr
Design Terry Paulhus

Every reasonable effort has been made to trace ownership and to obtain permission to reprint copyright material. The publishers would be pleased to have any errors or omissions brought to their attention so that they may be corrected in subsequent printings.

Weigl acknowledges Getty Images as its primary image supplier for this title.

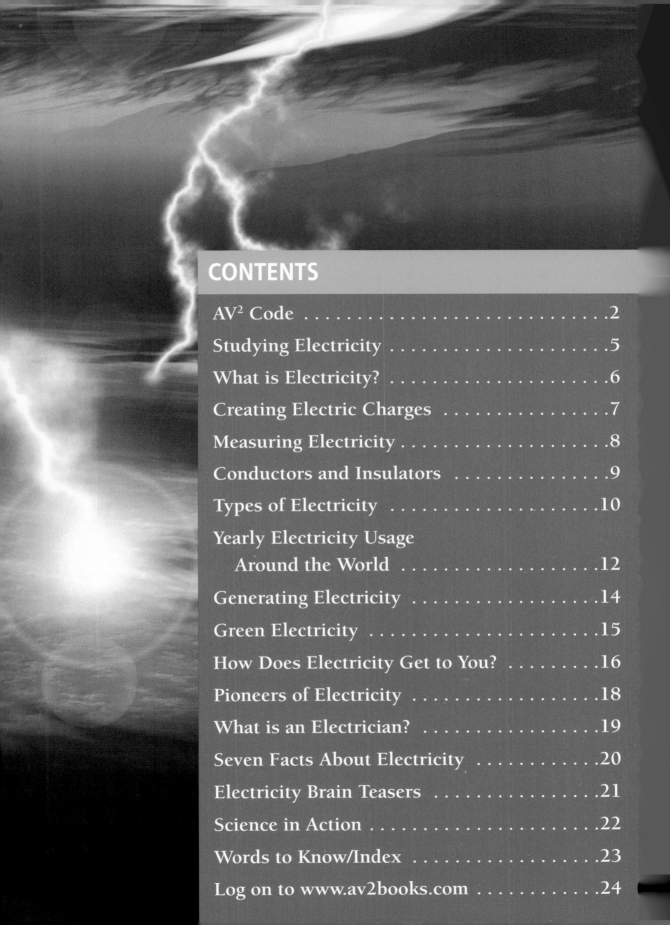

CONTENTS

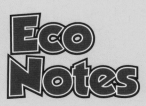

Lightning is caused by a buildup of electricity in clouds. During a thunderstorm, warm air moves up and cold air is forced down. This movement of warm and cold air causes **friction**. The friction creates positive and negative electric **charges** inside the cloud. The negative charges gather at the bottom of the cloud, and the positive charges move to the top. When a strong enough negative charge forms, it is attracted to the ground. The negative electric charges then move toward the ground. Positive electric charges in the ground move up to meet the negative charges from the cloud. When the two charges connect, lightning is formed.

Studying Electricity

Electricity can be found throughout the universe, including outer space, the stars, and the planets of Earth's solar system. There is even electricity in the human body. Every time a person's nerves send a message to his or her brain, it is in the form of electricity.

Electricity is one of the most commonly used types of **energy** in the world. It provides people with light, power, and heat. The use of electricity is so widespread that it is hard to believe it has only been widely used for a little more than 100 years.

■ Many touch screen devices rely on electricity to work. The electricity in the screen and the electricity in the person's hand create a connection at the place where the screen is touched.

What is Electricity?

Electricity is a type of energy. This energy can act in one of two ways. It can either build up in one place, or it can flow from one point to another.

ANATOMY OF AN ATOM

Electricity is made by **atoms**. Atoms are basic units of **matter** that make up almost everything. The **nucleus** of each atom is made up of particles with a positive charge, called protons, and particles with no charge, called neutrons. Circling around the nucleus are the electrons. Electrons are particles that have a negative charge.

Most atoms have the same number of electrons and protons. The positive and negative charges balance each other out. This means the atom has a neutral, or no, charge.

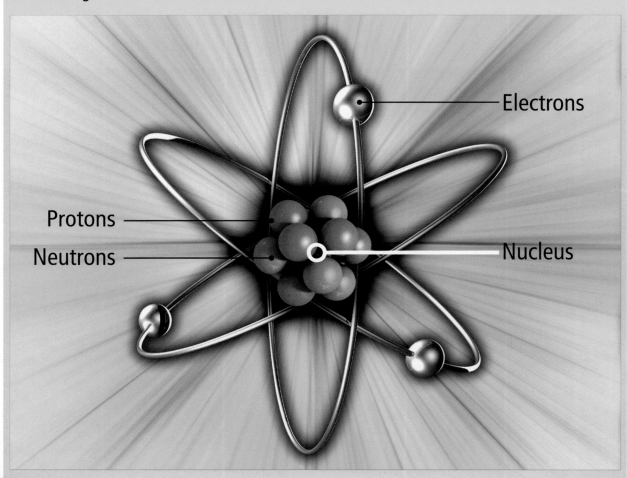

Electrons

Protons

Neutrons

Nucleus

Creating Electric Charges

Atoms with the same number of protons and electrons do not have a charge. These atoms are neutral. Some atoms have loosely held electrons. These electrons can separate from the atom. When this happens, the atom has more protons than electrons. The atom now has a positive charge. The electron that separated from the atom is called a free electron. If the free electron comes in contact with a neutral atom, it can join the atom. The atom now has a negative charge. When electrons move from one atom to another, the result is electricity.

For example, batteries contain many different atoms that come in contact with each other inside the battery. The contact causes electrons to move from one atom to another, creating electricity. This electricity is used to power electronic devices, such as cameras, music players, and cell phones.

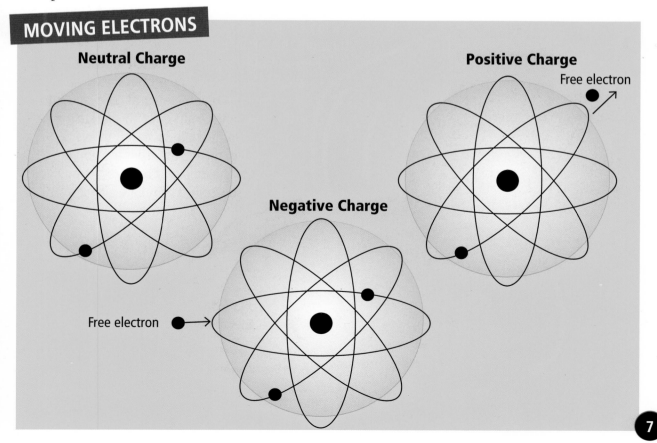

MOVING ELECTRONS

Neutral Charge

Positive Charge

Free electron

Negative Charge

Free electron

Measuring Electricity

Voltage is the electric force that causes free electrons to jump from one atom to another. The voltage itself does not move. Instead, it forces the electric **current** to move. A higher voltage will result in a greater electric current. Current is the movement of electricity. It is measured in **amperes**. A higher ampere means there is more flowing electricity.

Electricity flows like water. Imagine water flowing through a pipe. The flow of water is like the flow of electricity. Now, imagine a pump pushing the water through the pipe. The pump makes more water move through the pipe. This is like voltage moving more electricity in the electric current.

ELECTRICAL CIRCUITS

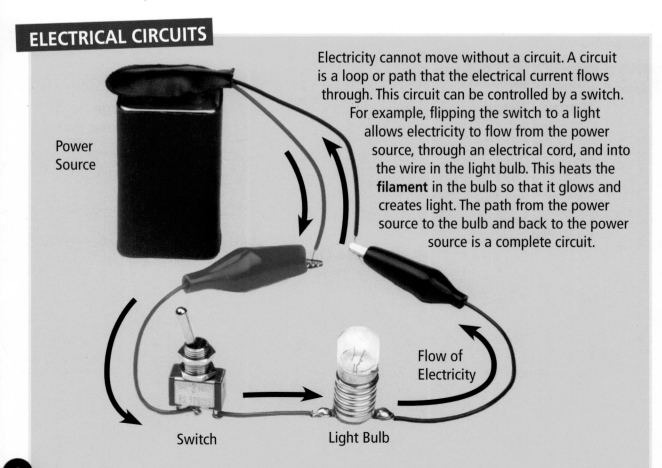

Electricity cannot move without a circuit. A circuit is a loop or path that the electrical current flows through. This circuit can be controlled by a switch. For example, flipping the switch to a light allows electricity to flow from the power source, through an electrical cord, and into the wire in the light bulb. This heats the **filament** in the bulb so that it glows and creates light. The path from the power source to the bulb and back to the power source is a complete circuit.

Power Source

Flow of Electricity

Switch

Light Bulb

Conductors and Insulators

Electricity can flow through some materials more easily than others. A **conductor** is a material that allows electricity to move through it. Conductors contain loosely held electrons. These electrons can move to other atoms to create an electric current. Some materials are better conductors than others. Metals, such as copper, gold, and silver, are good conductors. Without conductors, there would be no electricity in homes and schools, no computers, and no light bulbs. Conductors allow people to use electricity in many ways.

Insulators are the opposite of conductors. An insulator stops electrical currents from moving. Insulators have atoms with tightly held electrons that do not move to other atoms. Rubber, plastic, and glass are examples of insulators. Insulators are important because they allow people to use electricity safely. Electric wires, for example, are wrapped in rubber. The rubber stops the electricity from moving to other objects, such as a person's hand.

■ Light switches and electrical plugs are covered with plastic to make sure people do not get an electric shock from touching them.

SAFETY CHECK

Electricity can be very dangerous if not used responsibly.

- Never put anything except an electrical plug in a power outlet.

- Never handle appliances or electrical cords if you are wet or are standing in water.

- Never unplug electrical appliances by pulling on the cord. Pull from the plug.

- Never plug in more than two devices to an electrical outlet. This can cause fires.

Types of Electricity

There are two main types of electricity. These are static electricity and current electricity. Static electricity occurs when there is an imbalance of positive and negative charges in the atoms that make up an object.

STATIC ELECTRICITY

- Static electricity builds up in one place until it is released, or discharged. Static electricity often occurs with friction. For example, rubbing a balloon against a shirt will cause the balloon to stick to the shirt. This is because contact between the balloon and shirt separates the positive and negative charges. The shirt and the balloon now hold opposite charges. Opposite charges are attracted to each other, which makes the shirt and balloon stick together.

- Static electricity can also build up inside a person's body. A machine called a Van de Graaff generator can create static electricity inside a metal ball. When a person touches the ball, the static electricity moves to the person's body. The person's body then becomes charged. This can be seen in the person's hair. The hair stands up because the charges in each strand are the same. When the same charges are close, they push away from, or repel, each other.

Current electricity occurs when there is a constant flow of electrons. Current electricity works in two ways. **Alternating current (AC)** electricity travels in one direction. **Direct current (DC)** electricity can move in two directions.

CURRENT ELECTRICITY

Current electricity occurs when an electric charge moves from one place to another. All electric appliances run on current electricity. This type of electricity lasts longer than static electricity.

DIRECT CURRENT

Direct current is when all of the electrons in the electrical current move in the same direction. The amount of the charge can change, but the direction never does. Batteries are an example of direct current. The electricity always flows in the same direction, from the battery to the device the battery is powering.

ALTERNATING CURRENT

Alternating current is when the electrons change directions while flowing. The current changes direction back and forth repeatedly. The change of direction is known as frequency. The more times the current changes direction in one second, the higher the frequency. Alternating current is the type of electricity delivered through power lines to electrical outlets at home and school.

Yearly Electricity Usage Around the World

ARCTIC OCEAN

Canada
536 billion kWh

H

NORTH AMERICA

Continent: North America
Location: United States
Energy Use: 3.9 trillion **kilowatt hours (kWh)**
Fast Fact: The U.S. uses the most electricity in the world. More than 85 percent of its electricity is made from **fossil fuels**.

PACIFIC OCEAN

F

Mexico
181 billion kWh

F

ATLANTIC OCEAN

SOUTH AMERICA **H**

LEGEND

Main source of electricity:
F = Fossil Fuels
N = Nuclear Power
H = Hydropower

SCALE

621 Miles

0   1,000 Kilometers

N
W — E
S

Continent: South America
Location: Brazil
Energy Use: 404 billion kWh
Fast Fact: Brazil generates more than 95 percent of its electricity from **hydropower**.

WHAT HAVE YOU LEARNED ABOUT ELECTRICITY?

This map shows where the most electricity is used worldwide. Some parts of the world do not use as much electricity as others because they have little or no access to it. More than 25 percent of the world's population live without electricity.

1. Which countries use the most electricity?
2. Why is more electricity used in these areas?

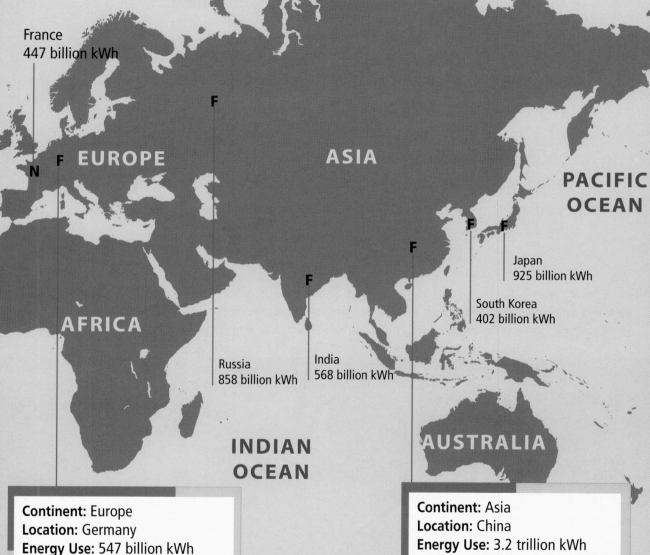

France
447 billion kWh

EUROPE

ASIA

PACIFIC OCEAN

Japan
925 billion kWh

South Korea
402 billion kWh

AFRICA

Russia
858 billion kWh

India
568 billion kWh

INDIAN OCEAN

AUSTRALIA

Continent: Europe
Location: Germany
Energy Use: 547 billion kWh
Fast Fact: Germany uses more electricity than any other country in Europe. Most of the country's electricity is made from burning coal.

Continent: Asia
Location: China
Energy Use: 3.2 trillion kWh
Fast Fact: China is the world's second largest consumer of electricity. From 2000 to 2008, China's electricity usage more than doubled.

SOUTHERN OCEAN

ANTARCTICA

Generating Electricity

Electricity is a secondary power source. This means that another energy source is used to create it. The main energy sources that create electricity often come in the form of water or hydropower, nuclear energy, and fossil fuels, such as coal, oil, and natural gas.

Most of the electricity people use is generated in a power plant. In the plant, steam is created by using an energy source such as coal. The steam is then directed into a turbine. As the steam passes through the turbine, it pushes fan blades inside the turbine and makes them spin. The spinning blades then have a kind of energy called mechanical energy. Then, another machine called a generator turns the mechanical energy into electricity.

■ Wind turbines can also produce electricity. Wind moves through the turbine blades, causing them to spin. Then, generators inside the turbine convert this movement into electricity.

Green Electricity

Coal, oil, and gas are **non-renewable** resources. Many countries produce about three-quarters of their electricity by burning non-renewable resources. This **pollutes** the air and contributes to **global warming**. Finding other ways to produce electricity and using less energy are two ways people can help reduce this pollution.

WIND ENERGY A wind turbine or windmill can be used to turn the power of the wind into electricity. When the wind blows, it pushes the blades on the windmill. This movement turns a turbine and creates electricity, which can be stored in batteries. This type of energy has been used for hundreds of years.

HYDROPOWER Electricity can be created from the power of water by using turbine blades. The water pushes the blades and the movement creates electricity.

SOLAR ENERGY The power from the heat of the Sun creates solar energy. This energy can be stored as electricity in solar cells and panels and used when needed.

GEOTHERMAL POWER Using steam from underground to drive a turbine is another way to use Earth's renewable resources to create electricity.

BIOMASS This process uses biological materials such as plants, trees, waste, and some types of garbage. These materials can be burned to produce steam in the same way that fossil fuels are used. The difference is these materials are renewable and produce less pollution when burned.

Eco Notes

Here are some other ways to use less electricity.
- Turn off lights, appliances, and electronics when not in use. Unplug anything that will not be used for a long period of time. Many devices use electricity even when they are not turned on.
- Wait until the dishwasher is full before turning it on.
- Keep the inside temperature at 68° Fahrenheit (20° Celsius) or lower. Try putting on a sweater instead of turning up the heat.
- Use low-energy or lower-watt light bulbs. A fluorescent bulb can use up to 75 percent less energy than a regular bulb.

How Does Electricity Get to You?

Electricity travels a long journey from the power plant where it is produced to the houses, schools, and other buildings where it is used.

1 Electricity is produced at a power plant. Different power plants use different methods to generate electricity.

2 Next, the electricity goes to a transformer. This is a device that raises the voltage to allow the electricity to travel long distances through power lines.

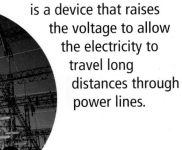

3 When the electricity has completed its long-distance journey, it arrives at a substation. Here, the voltage is lowered.

6 Finally, the electricity is ready to use. It arrives at homes, schools, and other buildings.

5 In order for the electricity to be sent into your home, it must go through another transformer. This transformer lowers the voltage, bringing it to a level that is usable by electric devices.

4 Power lines carry the electricity into the community where it can be used. These lines can be either aboveground on poles or underground in buried cables.

Eco Notes

Coming in contact with electrical wires can be dangerous. Less than one ampere of electricity can cause severe burns or even death. However, birds often land on electrical wires, and the electricity does not harm them. This is because electricity always takes a short and direct route to the ground. A bird on the wire does not provide a link to the ground, so the electricity stays in the wire.

Electricity Timeline

600 BC 1600 AD 1750 1785 1800 1810 1820 1830 1840 1850 1860 1870 1880 1890

1 **600 BC**
Static electricity is discovered by Greek philosopher Thales of Miletus.

2 **1600 AD**
An English scientist named William Gilbert creates the Latin term "electricus," which later becomes "electricity" in English.

3 **1752**
Benjamin Franklin proves that lightning is a form of electricity.

4 **1785**
French scientist Charles de Coulomb discovers that the area around an electric charge is also slightly electric. This is known as an **electric field**.

5 **1800**
Italian professor Alessandro Volta invents the battery. The volt is named after him.

6 **1820**
When he places a compass near an electric cable, Hans Christian Oerstad of Denmark discovers that electricity creates magnetism.

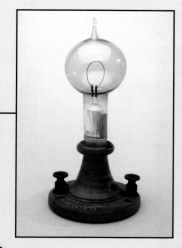

7 **1821**
The first electric motor is created in England by Michael Faraday.

8 **1827**
Georg Ohm realizes that certain metals are better for carrying electric charges than others. The measurement of resistance is named for him.

9 **1840**
James Prescott Joule proves that electricity is a type of energy. A measurement of energy, the joule, is named for him.

10 **1869**
The first large electric generators are designed by an engineer named Zenobe Gramme.

11 **1879**
Inventor Thomas Edison creates the first affordable, long-lasting light bulb.

12 **1882**
Thomas Edison opens the first electric power plants in the U.S. using his direct current system of electricity.

13 **1888**
Nikola Tesla invents the alternating current system of electricity. Tesla and Edison both competed with their systems, but Tesla's became the most commonly used.

Pioneers of Electricity

Thomas Edison

Thomas Edison is known for his many inventions. He is best known as the inventor of the light bulb. Edison had an idea to make light by heating a thin strip of material called a filament until it glowed. It took him more than a year, but in 1879 he was successful. The first light bulbs he created only lasted a few hours. By 1880, Edison had improved his design so that a bulb could burn for about 14 hours. The original Edison light bulbs look much like the light bulbs used today.

Benjamin Franklin

Benjamin Franklin was fascinated by the beauty and power of thunderstorms. He believed that lightning was electricity found in nature. In June 1752, Franklin decided to prove his theory. He attached a metal key to the tail of a kite and flew it during a thunderstorm. He hoped the metal key would attract the lightning and conduct electricity. It did. As well as changing human understanding of electricity, Franklin also created many of the common words used to describe electricity. These words include battery, charge, discharge, negative, positive, and electric shock.

What is an Electrician?

An electrician is someone who is specially trained to work with electrical systems, **electronics**, **circuit boards,** and wiring. Electricians are able to install, repair, maintain, and operate electrical equipment. Most electricians have four or five years of training. Many electricians work installing electrical wiring and systems in buildings and houses.

Electricians need special equipment to do their work. All kinds of screwdrivers, wire and bolt cutters, and wrenches are used. Measuring equipment, such as a volt or amp meter, is needed to tell how much electricity is running through a wire.

Nikola Tesla

Nikola Tesla (1856–1943) was a scientist who helped expand human understanding of electricity. A few of his accomplishments include fluorescent lighting and alternating current electricity. He also invented the Tesla coil, a type of transformer that produces a high voltage current at high frequencies. This creation led to inventions such as the radio and X-ray.

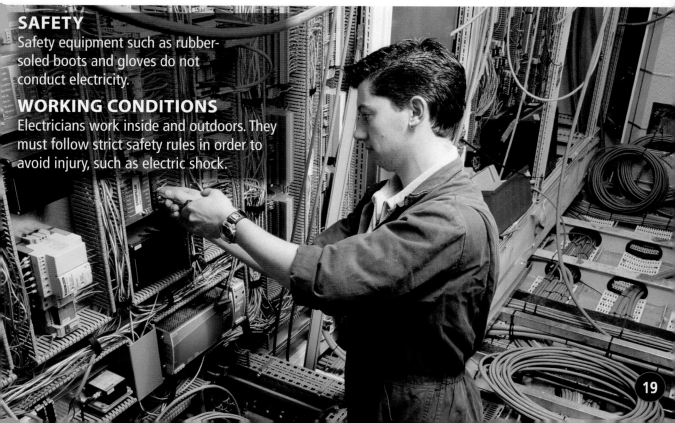

SAFETY
Safety equipment such as rubber-soled boots and gloves do not conduct electricity.

WORKING CONDITIONS
Electricians work inside and outdoors. They must follow strict safety rules in order to avoid injury, such as electric shock.

Seven Facts About Electricity

Information sent using electricity travels at about 186,000 miles (299,000 kilometers) per second.

There can be up to 3,000 volts of electricity in one spark of static electricity. The average battery is about 1.5 volts.

A lightning bolt may last only one second, but it can contain up to 3 million volts of electricity. That could keep 100 lamps lit for an entire day.

Manure contains a gas called methane, which can be burned to produce electricity.

An electric eel can carry as many as 600 volts of electricity. That is about five times the amount of electricity in a wall socket.

Hawai'i has one of the world's largest wind turbines. It is 20 stories tall. Each of its blades is as long as a football field.

If you place one million electrons side by side on the head of a pin, they would barely reach the other side.

Electricity Brain Teasers

1 All electricity comes from what tiny objects?

2 How long has electricity been in wide usage?

3 Where is the electricity used in homes and schools generated?

4 What is a conductor?

5 What is the difference between an electric charge and an electric current?

6 How is electric current measured?

7 What is the difference between AC and DC electricity?

8 What is an electron out of orbit called?

9 Which country consumes the most electricity?

10 How is the electrical power in a circuit measured?

ANSWERS: 1. Atoms 2. A little more than 100 years 3. At a power plant 4. A material that allows electricity to flow through it 5. An electric charge does not move, while electric current does. 6. In amps (amperes) 7. In AC, electricity changes directions, while in DC, electricity only goes one way 8. A free electron 9. The United States 10. In watts

Bending Water

Use the power of static electricity to bend water.

Tools Needed

A plastic comb   A sink and faucet with running water   Dry hair

Directions

1 Turn on the faucet so that you have a small stream of water flowing. It should be a steady stream.

2 Run the comb through dry hair about 10 times. You can also try rubbing the comb back and forth across a sweater.

3 Slowly bring the comb toward the stream of water. The comb must be close, but not touching.

4 What happens? Did the stream of water bend toward your comb?

Why Does This Happen?

Rubbing the comb through dry hair causes a build up of negatively charged electrons on the comb. The stream of water holds the opposite charge. When the comb is held near the water, the charge pulls the stream of water toward it. This causes the water to bend toward the comb.

Words to Know

alternating current (AC): an electric current that changes direction regularly

amperes: a measure of flowing electricity

atoms: the basic building blocks that make up everything in the observable universe

charges: electricity caused by an imbalance of either too many or too few electrons

circuit boards: boards on which electronic pathways are set

conductor: a material that allows electricity to pass through it

current: the flow of electricity

direct current (DC): an electric current that flows in one direction only

electric field: an invisible force that exists around electricity

electronics: devices and systems that use electricity to store and use information

energy: the ability to do work

filament: a thin, metal wire that glows when heated

fossil fuels: energy sources formed from the remains of living things over long period of time; includes coal and oil

friction: a force that acts against the movement of two objects in contact with each other

global warming: the increase in the average temperature on Earth

hydropower: electrical power produced by the movement of water

insulators: materials that do not allow electricity to pass through them

kilowatt hours (kWh): measure of energy used in one hour

matter: anything that has mass and takes up space

non-renewable: a type of energy that cannot be reused, such as fossil fuels

nucleus: the central or middle part of an atom.

pollutes: releases harmful substances

Index

Log on to www.av2books.com

AV² by Weigl brings you media enhanced books that support active learning. Go to www.av2books.com, and enter the special code found on page 2 of this book. You will gain access to enriched and enhanced content that supplements and complements this book. Content includes video, audio, web links, quizzes, a slide show, and activities.

Audio
Listen to sections of the book read aloud.

Video
Watch informative video clips.

Embedded Weblinks
Gain additional information for research.

Try This!
Complete activities and hands-on experiments.

WHAT'S ONLINE?

 Try This!

Test your knowledge about types of electricity.

Identify uses of electricity in the United States.

Add your own facts to the fact section.

Find out more about electricity through an educational activity.

 Embedded Weblinks

Review the basics of electricity.

Find more information about specific topics in electricity.

Explore interactive learning tools.

Learn more about uses of electricity in the United States.

Find out more about the history of electricity.

Read about an important scientist.

 Video

Watch a video introduction to electricity.

Watch another video about electricity.

EXTRA FEATURES

 Audio
Listen to sections of the book read aloud.

 Key Words
Study vocabulary, and complete a matching word activity.

 **Slide Show**
View images and captions and prepare a presentation

 Quizzes
Test your knowledge.

AV² was built to bridge the gap between print and digital. We encourage you to tell us what you like and what you want to see in the future.
Sign up to be an AV² Ambassador at www.av2books.com/ambassador.